Daily Life of the Ancient Egyptians

James F. Romano
The Brooklyn Museum

The Carnegie Museum of Natural History

This publication was made possible through a grant from the National Endowment for the Humanities, a federal agency.

Published by The Carnegie Museum of Natural History, Pittsburgh, PA 15213
Copyright © The Board of Trustees, Carnegie Institute, 1990
All rights reserved
Manufactured in the United States of America

ISBN 0-911239-18-9
Library of Congress Catalog Card Number: 89-85823

Front cover drawing: Anhorkhawy and his family. Detail of painting in tomb of Anhorkhawy (no. 359) at Thebes, Dynasty XX, reigns of Ramesses III and IV (ca. 1184–1147 B.C.).

Contents

About the Author iv

Introduction 1

The Family 3

Clothing, Jewelry, and Cosmetics 9

The Home and Its Furniture 22

Meals 32

Entertainment and Recreation 38

Popular Religion 45

Conclusion 49

Suggested Reading 50

Acknowledgments 52

About the Author

James F. Romano is Curator in the Department of Egyptian, Classical, and Ancient Middle Eastern Art at The Brooklyn Museum, where he has been employed since 1976. In addition to serving as an Adjunct Lecturer in the Art History Department at Queens College, he has been Chief Researcher in Egyptology at the C. G. Jung Foundation and Research Intern at The Metropolitan Musuem of Art. In the winter of 1989 he received his Ph.D. in Ancient Near Eastern and Egyptian Art and Archaeology from the Institute of Fine Arts at New York University. He is the author of numerous articles on ancient Egypt and coauthor of several catalogues of Egyptian art.

Archaeologists know more about the daily life of the Egyptians than any other ancient people. This understanding comes from three sources: representations of mundane activities on the walls of Egyptian tombs, artifacts discovered in ancient town sites and burials, and the words of the Egyptians themselves, who left us hundreds of documents describing their relationships with their family and neighbors, their legal transactions, and their attitudes toward ideal behavior.

Yet each type of evidence is by its nature somewhat imperfect. Daily life scenes on paintings and reliefs, for example, come exclusively from the tombs of the nobility. Because they preserve the aristocracy's view of Egyptian peasants and artisans, they probably present idealized versions of how most Egyptians lived. There is every reason to believe that the life of the common man and woman in Pharaonic Egypt was more difficult than these reliefs and paintings suggest.

Only a few town sites have ever been excavated in Egypt. In the last century Sir Flinders Petrie dug a small Middle Kingdom town at Lahun; the results of his excavations have never been thoroughly published. German and British Egyptologists working at el-Amarna, the site of Akhenaten's capital city, have unearthed private residences once inhabited by all strata of society from noblemen to the humblest peasants. However, their discoveries at el-Amarna tell us how Egyptians lived for only a relatively brief time span, the so-called Amarna Period (Dynasty XVIII, ca. 1347–1334 B.C.). Our most detailed knowledge of ancient daily life comes from the French excavations at Deir el-Medina, a village inhabited by workmen who labored in the Valley of the Kings and the Valley of the Queens across the Nile from the great city of Thebes.

Deir el-Medina was occupied for approximately four hundred years beginning in the reign of Tuthmosis I (ca. 1493–1481 B.C.), third ruler of the New Kingdom. Until more settlements such as Deir el-Medina are discovered, excavated, and published, Egyptologists will not know which aspects of life in that village are unique to the site and which are typical of Egypt as a whole.

The written record is of two types. One is a body of teachings commonly referred to as "wisdom literature." These documents relate how the Egyptians thought life *should* be lived. Temperance, diligence in all efforts, and respect for authority were among their most honored virtures. The other group of texts records correspondence and transactions between individuals. As valuable as these writings are for understanding certain aspects of ancient life, they are very specific and do not reveal all we might wish to know. Legal documents can tell the modern scholar, for example, that one house at Deir el-Medina contained two beds, but they give no clue as to what time an Egyptian went to sleep.

Yet if the available evidence is examined carefully, a reasonably accurate picture of the daily life of Pharaonic Egyptians emerges. Their lives were certainly ordered, but we never sense that they felt constrained by their rules or traditions. The Egyptians loved life and hoped to perpetuate its most pleasant aspects in the hereafter. Indeed, many of the objects illustrated in this volume were once used in life and subsequently buried in tombs to be used and enjoyed for eternity.

The Family

The nuclear family was the fundamental unit of ancient Egyptian society (figure 1). Until a child reached marriageable age—usually twenty or older for males, somewhat younger for females—he or she resided in the family home. A series of mutually beneficial relationships existed between the members of an Egyptian family. The father was responsible for the economic well-being of the group; however, he was obliged to honor his wife and not to question her authority in matters pertaining to her duties. The *Instructions of Ptahhotep*, an official from Dynasty V (ca. 2565–2423 B.C.), gives the following advice: "When you prosper and found your house, and love your wife with ardor, fill her belly, clothe her back, ointment soothes her body. Gladden her heart as long as you live; she is a fertile field for her lord" (Lichtheim, 1973:69). The wife supervised the household, including the servants, and cared for the upbringing of the children who, in turn, owed their mother and father strict obedience. When parents reached the advanced stage of their lives, children were expected to help them as their "staff of old age." Children's final responsibilities to their parents were to bury them in accordance with strict religious practice and to leave offerings at their graves.

An Egyptian household might also encompass an extended family. If a man married before he was financially independent, the young couple might move in with the bride's parents. Because the Egyptians had an extraordinary regard for the elderly, grandparents often lived with their adult children and grandchildren, no doubt helping to perpetuate the traditional

1. *Nykare, a Dynasty V official, and his family.*

Limestone. Height, 57.5 cm. Dynasty V (ca. 2565–2423 B.C.). Saqqara? The Brooklyn Museum 49.215, Charles Edwin Wilbour Fund.

aspect of all Egyptian life. Pharaonic art often reflects the Egyptians' respect for ancestors. Many homes at Deir el-Medina contained sculptures thought to be images of a divinity that commemorated dead relations (figure 2), and funerary stelae frequently mention the deceased's lineage, extending back several generations (figure 3).

Many marriages were arranged by parents, but the tone of much Egyptian love poetry shows that many couples felt genuine passion and affection for each other. Marriage ceremonies per se did not exist in ancient Egypt. When a couple decided to live together as husband and wife, one of the partners simply moved in with the other. As casual as this relationship may seem, Egyptian marriages involved complex legal arrangements. Before establishing a household, the man and woman entered into a marriage contract. Each party determined what possessions he or she brought into the union, so in the event of divorce ownership could not be disputed. Similarly, any property inherited by one of the partners during the marriage was declared the sole property of the recipient. A common clause in written contracts required the man to bestow a gift on his bride as compensation for the loss of her virginity.

Marriages were dissolved by a simple repudiation of the union initiated by either husband or wife. Common grounds for divorce included adultery, infertility, and overall antipathy. Egyptian tradition required that the dissolution of a marriage be accompanied by a divorce agreement which contained a clause that the rejected partner was henceforth free to remarry. If a man left his wife for any reason but adultery, he was obliged to pay her a lump sum equivalent to one-third of his property plus a "divorce penalty." A house that belonged to the woman before the marriage remained hers, and the

2. Bust found in a Deir el-Medina home.

Limestone. Height 26.2 cm. Dynasty XIX (ca. 1295–1185 B.C.). Deir el-Medina. The Brooklyn Museum 54.1, Charles Edwin Wilbour Fund.

3. Stela that belonged to the Overseer of the Storehouse, Kemtu. The inscription also identifies his wife It, other members of his family, and several servants.

Painted limestone. Height 73.3 cm; width 42 cm; thickness 14 cm. Dynasty XII (ca. 1979–1801 B.C.). Abydos? CMNH 21538-38.

man was obliged to vacate; otherwise, she had to relinquish all claims to the home. The economic hardships that such regulations created meant that divorce was rare and most Egyptian marriages remained lifetime relationships.

A woman's right to ownership of property codified in these contracts was simply one aspect of her legal, economic, and social status in ancient Egypt. Although women never played a dominant role in the Egyptian bureaucracy, many held official titles that imply administrative and religious duties including "Overseer of the Storehouse of Royal Linen," "Funerary Priestess," and "Scribe." Like men, women could inherit property and bequeath it in their wills; they could initiate law suits and testify in judicial proceedings. Literacy among upper-class Egyptian women is well documented.

The primary purpose of any marriage was the perpetuation of the family line through children. Statues and reliefs suggest that young children spent most of their time naked (figure 1); their heads were shaved except for a long braided sidelock.

Although Egyptian children had toys and are occasionally depicted at play, much of their time was spent in preparing for the day when they would be viewed as adults. Peasant children accompanied their parents into the fields, while male offspring of craftsmen often served as apprentices to their fathers. Girls often learned to run households. More privileged children received formal education leading, it was hoped, to a career as a scribe. Temples often maintained schools where priests taught promising youngsters; children of the nobility sometimes received private instruction from tutors.

4. Close-up of a piece of linen probably intended as a bandage, illustrating a closely woven plainweave. Linen. Complete piece: width 14.5–14.8 cm; length 250 cm. New Kingdom or later (ca. 1539–30 B.C.). Provenience unknown. CMNH 17045-14a.

Clothing, Jewelry, and Cosmetics

The ancient Egyptians made much of their clothing from linen, a lightweight material affording them great comfort on warm days (figure 4). As early as 3000 B.C., Egyptian weavers produced linen textiles much finer than the modern linen handkerchief. By the New Kingdom (ca. 1539–1070 B.C.), weavers were using two distinct types of looms, the horizontal ground variety and the vertical two-beamed form, no doubt imported from the ancient Near East. The resulting linen was made into simple garments that were wrapped around the body and tied in place or supported by straps. Sewing played little part in the manufacture and wearing of ancient Egyptian clothing.

Since Egyptian evenings are sometimes quite cool, particularly during the winter, the ancient Egyptians needed warm clothing, especially cloaks, and made much of it from wool. The frequent representations of sheep on the walls of Egyptian tombs show that Egyptian wool was a domestic product and was not imported.

Garments were almost always white. Patterned clothing was extremely rare; pleating provided the only break in the uniformity of the surface. The pleating process, however, remains unknown. Some scholars have suggested that the cloth was pressed into a grooved board and the resulting ridges fixed into the garment with sizing. Others believe that the pleats were made entirely by hand and reset each time the garment was washed.

Quite naturally, clothing styles changed over time. In the Old Kingdom (ca. 2750–2250 B.C.), for example, noblemen usually wore a kilt made of a rectangular piece of linen wrapped around the waist (figure 1). By the Middle Kingdom (ca. 2025–1627/1606 B.C.), this kilt had evolved into an undergarment, over which the Egyptian male sported a long, transparent skirt reaching halfway down the calf. In general, the tendency among the Egyptian aristocracy was away from austere costuming and toward fussy, elaborate attire. One of the periods of *haute couture* occurred during the reign of Amenhotep III (ca. 1390–1352 B.C.) in Dynasty XVIII. Women's fashions were particularly elegant at that time. A typical dress consisted of a sheet of fringed and pleated linen, six feet long and three feet wide, that was first wrapped around the torso, then draped over a shoulder, and finally tied with a sash resting beneath a bare breast (figure 5).

5. Lady Thepu.

Painted gesso. Height 30.2 cm. Late Dynasty XVIII (ca. 1390–1352 B.C.). Thebes. The Brooklyn Museum 65.197, Charles Edwin Wilbour Fund.

Workers who labored in the fields had little use for such stylish excesses. They wore simple kilts or nothing at all. Headgear was extremely rare in ancient Egypt, except as part of royal regalia or in the form of headbands called fillets. Perhaps the only nonroyal group that regularly wore some type of head covering were winnowers. Several New Kingdom tomb paintings showing harvesting scenes include vignettes of winnowers, their heads encased in loosely tied kerchiefs with long queues that fall onto their backs. This unusual headcloth was probably intended to prevent the chaff from becoming entangled in their hair.

The Egyptians seem to have spent most of their time barefoot. When footgear was required, they donned a pair of sandals usually made of woven or plaited grasses. The wealthiest Egyptians wore sandals made of leather. Most sandals featured a thong that passed between the first and second toes and extended over the instep, forming a Y-shaped harness. The rules of etiquette required Egyptians to remove their sandals in the presence of a superior. Only rarely do we find representations of an Egyptian wearing sandals while worshiping a god.

The stark whiteness of the Egyptians' clothing served as an ideal backdrop for their multicolored jewelry. The finest examples were made of gold and silver with inlays of semiprecious stones such as turquoise, lapis lazuli, and carnelian. The lower strata of society wore cheaper costume jewelry of steatite or faience (sand kneaded with water and a binding agent) covered with blue or green glaze imitating lapis lazuli or turquoise.

Although the Egyptians wore jewelry as ornaments, they regarded their necklaces, armlets, earrings, and so forth as having magical powers. Sometimes the form of an object, such as an amulet (figure 6), conveyed

6. Necklace with amulets representing the deities Isis and Horus, Bes, and Ptah-Sokar, as well as fish, a cat, and a wedjet-eye. Faience and carnelian. Length 35 cm. Early Dynasty XVIII (ca. 1479–1425 B.C.). Abydos, D116. CMNH 1917-31.

the piece's protective intent. The aperture of the cowrie shell (figure 7) may have suggested the opening of a woman's vagina, since the Egyptians associated this form with fertility and used it on girdles and other items worn by maidens. Even the material from which jewelry was made had special meanings. The Egyptians saw gold, for example, as a reflection of the glorious, life-giving properties of the sun, while associating deep blue lapis lazuli with the Nile.

Throughout the history of ancient Egypt, the most common ornament was the simple necklace made of a single strand of beads, sometimes interspersed with amulets (figure 6). Archaeologists have discovered necklaces with shell, steatite, and copper beads in graves of the Predynastic Period (ca. 4500–3100 B.C.). Later examples feature amulets, balls, cowrie shells, disks, rings, and barrel-shaped beads. Those Egyptians who could afford more elaborate neckwear favored a broad collar made of rows of faience beads (figure 5). Called *wesekh* ("the broad one") by the Egyptians, these fancy collars probably copied garlands of flowers, berries, and leaves.

The Egyptians wore a wide variety of limb ornaments, including armlets, wristlets, and anklets, the form and material of which depended on the wealth of the owner. Royalty and nobility favored ornate gold jewelry with incised or inlaid decoration. Common folk contented themselves with modest pieces made of rows of shell, ivory, and faience beads. A similar distinction was made in the wearing of finger rings. The wealthy adorned themselves with gold and silver examples often decorated with an image of a king or god; cheaper faience versions were common among the workers at el-Amarna and Deir el-Medina.

Earrings were a relatively late addition to the in-

7. Necklace with cowrie shell beads.

Faience, steatite, and shell. Length 33 cm. Early Dynasty XVIII (ca. 1479– 1425 B.C.). Abydos, D116. CMNH 1917-56.

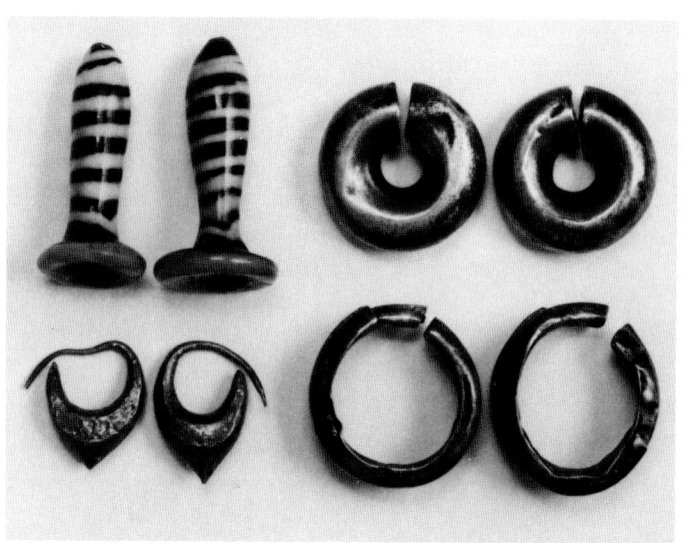

8. Earrings including studs and several hoop styles.

Clockwise from top left: All early Dynasty XVIII (ca. 1479–1425 B.C.) except ear studs. Ear studs: *Glass. Diameter approx. 1.8 cm; length approx. 3.1 cm. Dynasty XVIII (ca. 1539–1295 B.C.). Provenience unknown. CMNH Z9-498a and b.* Penannular: *Silver or electrum. Diameter 2 cm; thickness 7 mm. Abydos, D102. CMNH 1917-155 and 156.* Ribbed penannular: *Gold. Diameter approx. 2 cm; thickness 6–8 mm. Abydos, D102. CMNH 1917-152 and 154.* Leech-type: *Gold over core. Height 1.5–1.6 cm; width 1.4 cm. Abydos, D116. CMNH 1917-49 and 50.*

ventory of ancient Egyptian jewelry. A few examples have been found in contexts contemporary with Dynasty XII (ca. 1979–1801 B.C.) and XIII (ca. 1801–1627/1606 B.C.), but only in Dynasty XVIII (ca. 1539–1295 B.C.) did earrings became common. The most popular variety was the hoop or penannular form (figure 8), although so-called tube-and-boss earrings are also well documented. Men, women, and children all wore earrings during the New Kingdom, but this form of jewelry seems to have been an extravagant accessory, used only by the aristocracy.

Two unusual variations of the earring developed in the New Kingdom: the ear stud and the ear plug. A stud (figure 8) consists of a circular head, either flat or domed, with a projecting shaft. The Egyptians inserted the shaft through a hole in the ear lobe, allowing the round head to rest in the ear. Ear studs made of stone, metal, glass, and faience survive from antiquity. Ear plugs are large disks, each with a deep channel along the edge; they were fitted into holes of enormous proportions punched in the ear lobes. Plugs seem to have been inspired by trends in Nubian fashion during Dynasty XVIII.

On special occasions such as banquets, Egyptian women wore fillets on their heads (figure 5). Most consisted of strands of flowers, although permanent examples made of metal with semiprecious stone inlays are also known.

The Egyptians treasured their jewelry and took considerable care to see that each piece was carefully protected. The wealthy often stored it in wooden chests; simple baskets or small trinket boxes were used to house more modest collections (figure 9).

The ancient Egyptians took great care to protect their skin from the drying effects of sun, wind, and sand. At least once a day they rubbed their bodies with some variety of scented oil or unguent. The rich used expensive imported lotions from the Levant, which they stored in fancy vessels like the small jar in figure 10; individuals of more modest wealth could afford only castor bean oil. Hair was also subject to damage by Egypt's arid climate. The Egyptians treated their tresses with a moistened cream that they molded into a

9. Small, lidded basket and decorated wooden box that is missing its lid.

Basket: Rushes and palm leaves. Height 7 cm; diameter 15.5 cm. Probably New Kingdom (ca. 1539–1070 B.C.). Provenience unknown. CMNH 9074-2408a and b. Box: Painted? wood. Height 5.7 cm; width 7.5 cm; length 7.1 cm. Roman Period (ca. 30 B.C.–A.D. 395). Faiyum. CMNH 2231-27.

conical lump of tallow impregnated with myrrh. They wore these cones on the tops of their heads (figure 5).

Cosmetics had been a standard feature of the Egyptian toilette since the Badarian Period (ca. 4500–3800 B.C.). People of that remote age left pieces of malachite, a copper oxide that was crushed and applied as green eye paint, in simple graves for use in the afterlife. By the Old Kingdom, the Egyptians wore both green and black eye makeup. The latter, called kohl, was made from galena, a sulfate of lead. Kohl had the effect of cutting down the sun's intense glare; it was also mentioned in medical papyri as part of prescriptions against diseases of the eye. By Dynasty XVIII, kohl superseded its green counterpart as the preferred eye makeup.

10. Cosmetic containers and cosmetic spoon. The kohl pot (far left) still has traces of black eye paint (galena?) inside.

Clockwise from left: All early Dynasty XVIII (ca. 1479–1425 B.C.); Abydos, D116 except alabastron. Kohl pot: Calcite. Height 6.3 cm; diameter 4.8 cm. CMNH 1917-84. Monkey holding kohl tube: *Painted limestone.* Height 9.3 cm; width 3 cm; length 5.8 cm. CMNH 1917-2. (See also figure 27.) Triple kohl tube with climbing monkey: *Wood and bone.* Height 16 cm; width 7.5 cm; depth 3.4 cm. CMNH 1917-4. Small jar: *Faience.* Height 5.8 cm; diameter 3.9 cm. CMNH 1917-535. Alabastron: *Glass.* Height 11.2 cm; diameter 3.3 cm. Late Period (ca. 664–332 B.C.). Provenience unknown. CMNH 29825. Spoon: *Wood.* Length 7.6 cm; width 3.7 cm. CMNH 1917-16.

Powdered eye makeup was stored in small, portable containers. During the Old and Middle Kingdoms, the standard kohl pot was a small stone jar, usually squat, with a wide rim, small mouth, and low, flat lid (figure 10). Beginning in Dynasty XVIII, however, the creative predilections of Egyptian artisans extended to the design of kohl containers. Some pots took the shape of palmiform or papyriform capitals; others com-

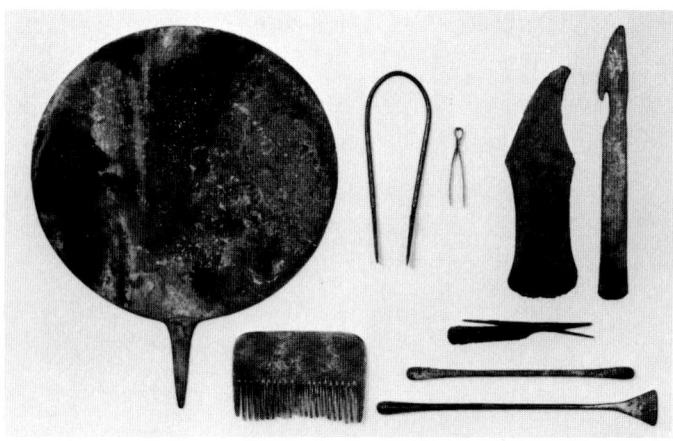

11. Toilette equipment.
Clockwise from left: All early Dynasty XVIII (ca. 1479–1425 B.C.) except hair implement. Mirror with handle missing: *Bronze*. Height 20.2 cm; width 16.8 cm. Abydos, D116. CMNH 1917-14. Tweezers: *Bronze*. Length 10.5 cm; width 3.8 cm (large) and length 4.4 cm; width 1 cm (small). Abydos, D119. CMNH 1917-231 (large) and 231a (small). Razors: *Bronze*. Length 12.5 cm; width 4 cm (left) and length 14.6 cm; width 1.7 cm (right). Abydos, D116 (left) and D102 (right). CMNH 1917-17 (left) and 17a (right). Hair implement: *Bronze*. Length 8.2 cm; width 1.5 cm. Dynasty XVIII (ca. 1539-1295 B.C.). Hu, Y53. CMNH 1234-16. Kohl sticks: *Bronze*. Length 12.5 cm; width 8 mm (top) and length 15.5 cm; width 2 cm (bottom). Abydos, D116. CMNH 1917-6 (top) and 21 (bottom). Comb: *Horn*. Height 5 cm; width 7.5 cm. Abydos, D116. CMNH 1917-24.

bined two or more tubes in a single piece (figure 10). A charming class of kohl pots from the first half of Dynasty XVIII shows a pet monkey standing and proffering a kohl container (figure 10). Men and women applied kohl by moistening either their finger or a rod, called a kohl stick (figure 11), in water or oil kept in a spoon (figure 10). They then dipped the wet surface into the kohl and carefully dabbed it onto their faces.

The Egyptians used red ocher, an iron oxide, in a fatty or gum-resin base to color their cheeks and perhaps also their lips. They occasionally highlighted their hair with henna, a reddish-brown dye. Henna is sometimes also found on the nails and on the soles of the feet of mummies. Egyptologists are not sure, however, if these traces indicate coloring used in life or if they are simply stains from the mummification process. Perfumes, in the form of scented oils and fats, were used at least as early as Dynasty XVIII. The Egyptians stored their perfumes in small vases made of multicolored glass (figure 10).

Occasionally statues or tomb reliefs show a man with a thin moustache or a short, neatly groomed chin beard, but as a rule the Egyptians were clean shaven. Unsightly stubble was permissible only during a period of mourning. To shave, men used copper or bronze razors with short handles (figure 11), after applying oil or unguent to the face to soften the skin and beard. The Egyptians pulled out any stray hairs with tiny tweezers (figure 11). Professional barbers called *chaku* ("shavers") served the wealthy. The average Egyptian man, however, probably tended to his own tonsorial needs on a daily basis.

Because of the intense heat of the Egyptian sun, many men and women preferred to have their heads shaved or to wear their hair very short. On public occasions they covered their heads with wigs, made of approximately three hundred braids, each with four hundred or more human hairs. Statues and tomb reliefs often represent members of the Egyptian elite adorned with ornate wigs (figure 5). The actual examples that survive from antiquity, however, are far simpler than these depictions, suggesting that artisans may have exaggerated the complexity of the wigs for aesthetic reasons. The Egyptians who chose to keep their hair relatively long cared for it with wood or ivory combs (figure 11) and held it in place with hairpins.

While tending to their personal grooming, Egyptian men and women used mirrors with metal disks polished to a high sheen (figure 11). Mirror handles took on many forms during the three millennia of Pharaonic culture. Among the more common handle motifs are papyrus columns, female figures, images of minor deities, and heads of the goddess Hathor.

The Home and Its Furniture

The Egyptians built the walls of their houses from sun-dried mud bricks. The choice of this inexpensive material meant that houses could be erected quickly. Mud brick, however, was highly susceptible to erosion and natural deterioration; and even in Egypt's arid climate, the life span of these houses was probably not more than two or three generations. Ceilings consisted of layers of wooden poles and sticks laid crosswise on palm rafters. Palm logs supported the ceilings of large rooms. In an effort to reduce the spread of dust, the Egyptians placed reed matting on their pressed-earth floors. Windows were situated high on the wall, facilitating the escape of heat; stone grills on these windows afforded security, especially from pesky birds.

The size and appearance of an Egyptian house depended on the family's wealth and the location of the building. In antiquity, as today, urban land was scarce.

12. *An urban dwelling belonging to a member of the New Kingdom aristocracy. Drawing copied from a painting in Djheutynefer's tomb, mid Dynasty XVIII (ca. 1427–1400 B.C.), Thebes.*

Structures built in one of ancient Egypt's major cities were smaller than their counterparts in the suburbs or in spacious country settings.

Paintings on the walls of Dynasty XVIII tombs found across the river from ancient Thebes give a good idea of an urban residence belonging to a member of the New Kingdom aristocracy (figure 12). These multistory structures resemble town houses of the nineteenth century. Servants lived and worked in the basement, where they prepared food and executed tasks such as weaving fabric and grinding grain. A staircase led from the street to the first floor, where the ceilings were the

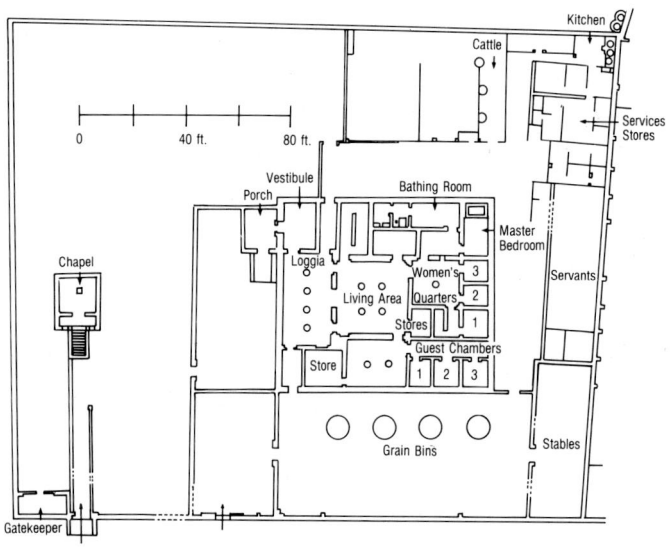

13. Plan of a typical country mansion in the suburbs of el-Amarna, late Dynasty XVIII (ca. 1347–1334 B.C.).

highest in the house. The principal room of the house was usually found on this main floor. In this "living room" the owner relaxed, the family dined, and on special occasions guests were received and entertained. The private quarters of the house, including the bedrooms, were situated on the upper floors.

Ventilators on the roof provided fresh air to the top story. A rooftop terrace no doubt afforded family members a place of nighttime refuge, where they could enjoy the delightful breezes blowing off the desert.

Outside the city, nobles' houses were far more expansive, often featuring elegant gardens with shade trees and pools filled with an array of fish and fowl. Some of the largest and best-preserved country mansions were found in the suburbs of Akhenaten's capital city at el-Amarna. Most had only a single story. A standard example, shown in figure 13, is surrounded by a rectangular wall against which servants' quarters, work areas, the kitchen, stables, and cattle pens were constructed. Entrance to the house proper was through a porch and vestibule, which gave access to a broad, columned hall called a loggia. Adjacent to it was a spacious, normally square room. This was the equivalent of the living room of the urban town house. The high ceilings, supported by palm columns, probably featured clerestory windows that gave the hall extra air and light. Sleeping quarters for children and guests were normally found just off this hall. The master bedroom was distinguished from all other chambers in the mansion by the presence of a small alcove for the bed. The walls of this alcove were unusually thick, suggesting that the area above the bed was vaulted. If so, openings in the vault would have allowed for additional ventilation.

Cleanliness was extremely important to the fastidious Egyptians, so it is not surprising that many of the mansions at el-Amarna had elaborate bathing and lavatory facilities. The bathroom was normally situated just off the master bedroom; it consisted of a low mud-brick wall sheathed in limestone with a limestone floor. The bather stood on this floor while attendants poured water over his or her body. Animal or vegetable oils mixed with powdered limestone served as cleansing agents. Excess water flowed into a pottery vessel that was emptied after bathing. A typical Egyptian latrine was composed of a wood, clay, or, in the wealthiest households, limestone toilet seat that rested on a sand-filled pot.

The houses of Egypt's "working class" were far more modest than the town houses or the el-Amarna mansions. In its final form, the village of Deir el-

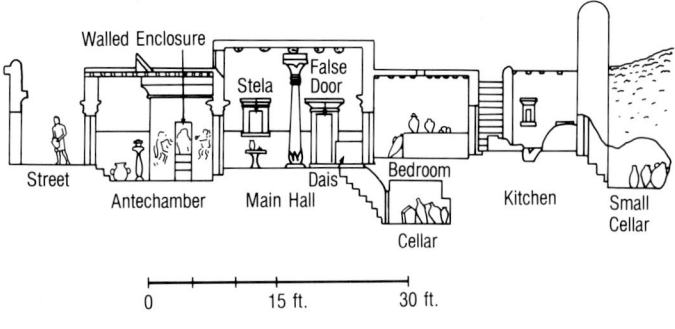

14. Section of a typical worker's house in Deir el-Medina, Dynasty XIX (ca. 1295–1185 B.C.).

Medina contained approximately seventy houses arranged along narrow streets. The entire village was surrounded by a thick enclosure wall. Most of the Deir el-Medina houses were long and narrow, ranging from approximately thirty to eighty feet in length and twelve to eighteen feet in width. The thinness of the walls indicates that each house consisted of a single story.

One entered a typical house at Deir el-Medina (figure 14) by stepping down from street level into a square antechamber. Most of these rooms featured an unusual walled enclosure, approximately two feet off the ground, that was reached by a set of mud-brick steps. The French Egyptologists who excavated Deir el-Medina thought these enclosures once accommodated beds that were used for childbirth. It is unlikely that so much space in the cramped interiors of the Deir el-Medina houses would have been intended exclusively for an event that happened only once a year. Although these boxed beds may have been used as a "delivery room," they probably served on a daily basis as the principal sleeping area of the house. By placing the bed well above ground level, the residents of Deir el-Medina probably helped to deter dangerous creatures, such as snakes and scorpions, that wandered into the house at night. Many of these enclosed areas were decorated with representations of gods, including Bes, who served as guardians of the residence particularly during the perilous hours between dusk and dawn. Antechambers often also contained small chapels with niches for stelae and sculpted busts, perhaps representing the family's deceased ancestors (figure 2).

The antechamber led, via a short flight of stairs, to the so-called main hall, the largest room in the house, which always had at least one supporting column. A stela and a niche shaped like a door, which Egyptologists call a false door, for the domestic cult were usually found in this room. Another typical feature was a low dais made of mud brick bordered by limestone blocks and set against one of the walls. Plastered and whitewashed, the dais may have served as the eating area. A set of stairs, hidden by a trapdoor, ran from this main hall down to a small cellar where the family's stores were kept in pottery jars. On one side of the dais was a door that opened into a small room, perhaps a bedroom for the children. On the other side, a second door gave access to a passageway leading to a small courtyard that functioned as the kitchen. Here, standard cooking equipment, including a clay oven, a grain silo, and a flat stone surface for kneading bread, was built into the floor and walls. Some of the houses at Deir el-Medina had a second, smaller cellar extending into the bedrock. A staircase led from the kitchen to the roof where the inhabitants of these houses found relief from their crowded, poorly ventilated quarters.

Egyptian houses were filled with a wide variety of

superbly designed and crafted furniture. Egyptian carpenters rarely worked in native woods such as acacia, sycamore fig, and tamarask, which they found ill-suited for their purposes. Instead, they used imported woods including ash, beech, elm, fir, juniper, maple, oak, pine, plum, and yew from Syria. Trading expeditions to Lebanon brought back coveted cedar wood; and ebony, native to Nubia, was used for furniture of the highest quality.

The most common piece of furniture in an ancient Egyptian home was the low stool (figure 15) made with simple wood, leather, or woven-rush seats. The finest examples have contoured frames for more comfortable seating. Most Egyptian stools feature four legs, although a simpler, three-legged variety was used primarily while working. Often the legs of stools and other pieces of furniture were carved to represent the legs of animals, including the lion and bull. For convenient storage and transport, carpenters designed a folding stool, which closed like a modern director's chair.

In Egypt chairs were luxury items found primarily in homes of the wealthy. The classic Egyptian chair (figure 16) had animal legs, a rush seat, and a slanted, frequently contoured back reinforced from behind by vertical supports. Chairs were frequently embellished with decorations ranging from simple geometric inlays to scenes with ornate figures carved in raised relief and occasionally gilded.

Tables, which tended to be low, were used for eating and working (figure 17). A common form evokes the facade of an Egyptian temple, with the table's splayed legs recalling the shape of the temple pylon and the cavetto-and-torus cornice.

Poor Egyptians slept on the reed mats placed on the bare ground or mud-brick platforms. Their wealthier

15. *A stool, the most common piece of furniture in ancient Egypt.*
Wood. Height 24.5 cm. Dynasty XIX (ca. 1295–1185 B.C.). Saqqara. The Brooklyn Museum 37.45E, Charles Edwin Wilbour Fund.

neighbors, however, enjoyed the comfort of beds, which were low and slightly sloping, and consisted of a wooden frame supported by four legs (figure 18). The "springs" were a single layer of woven rush that gave the bed some play; folded linen served as the "mattress." The ancient Egyptian equivalent of a pillow was

16. A typical Egyptian chair.

Wood. Height 90 cm. Late Dynasty XVIII (ca. 1390–1352 B.C.). Thebes? The Brooklyn Museum 37.40E, Charles Edwin Wilbour Fund.

17. A table. Its design represents a temple pylon.

Wood. Height 29.9 cm. Early Dynasty XVIII (ca. 1479–1425 B.C.). Provenience unknown. The Brooklyn Museum 37.41E, Charles Edwin Wilbour Fund.

a wooden headrest in the form of a curved support atop a column (figure 19). Sleepers rested their heads in the support, probably while lying on their sides. The Egyptians sometimes tempered the hardness of the headrest by winding several layers of thick linen around the support.

The ancient Egyptians did not have cupboards or chests of drawers. Instead, they stored their clothing and household furnishings, such as bedding, in wooden boxes or, more commonly, in baskets. These containers were frequently placed beneath the bed.

Every Egyptian house needed a supply of oil lamps. The Egyptians rose before sunrise and, no doubt, were

18. *Statuette of a female resting on a bed.*

Limestone. Height 8.3 cm; width 6 cm; length 16.9 cm. Dynasty XVIII (ca. 1539– 1295 B.C.). The Metropolitan Museum of Art 15.2.8, Rogers Fund, 1915.

active in the early hours of the evening. To illuminate their homes, the poor used simple lamps consisting of a bowl with a wick (figure 20). More elaborate lamps were placed on stands.

Meals

Every Egyptian home had a supply of simple wheel-made pottery used for storing, preparing, and serving food. Grains and other nonperishable commodities were kept in large jars (figure 21) often located in cellars near the kitchen. To guard against petty thievery by servants, wealthy Egyptians would place over the mouth of the storage vessel a pottery saucer

19. Headrest.

Wood. Height 20.5 cm;
width 22.5 cm; depth 7.7 cm.
New Kingdom (ca. 1539–
1070 B.C.). Provenience
unknown. CMNH 21538-14.

that they tied in place by knotting a linen cloth around the jar neck. They covered the knot with a mass of clay or wax stamped with the name of the owner. A would-be thief could not disturb the contents of the jar without first destroying this seal. Strangely, these jars usually have pointed bottoms that prevented them from standing on their own. Representations usually show them leaning against walls or set into simple rings serving as pottery stands.

20. Lamp.

Ceramic. Height 2.5 cm; width 7 cm; length 7.7 cm. New Kingdom (ca. 1539–1070 B.C.)? Provenience unknown. CMNH 19458-7.

Most Egyptian homes were equipped with a cylindrical, baked-clay stove about three feet high with a small opening on the bottom to create a draft and to allow for easy collection of ashes. Wood, charcoal, or dried manure, ignited by a simple bow drill, served as fuel. The basic piece of cooking equipment was a two-handled pottery saucepan which the cook placed on the stove. If a stove was not available, the saucepan was balanced on a tripod set over an open fire.

21. Painted ceramic vessels that could have appeared on a New Kingdom table.

Left to right: All early Dynasty XVIII (ca. 1479–1425 B.C.). Jug with handle: Height 14.8 cm; diameter 8.3 cm. Abydos, D116. CMNH 1917-500. Mug: Height 14.3 cm; diameter 4.6 cm. Abydos, D102. CMNH 1917-383. Large jar: Height 28.5 cm; diameter 9.5 cm. Abydos, D116. CMNH 1917-413. Shallow bowl: Height 4.2 cm; diameter 12 cm. Abydos, D119. CMNH 1917-417. Large bowl: Height 9.2 cm; diameter 29.8 cm. Abydos, D102. CMNH 1917-496. Small jar: Height 7.8 cm; diameter 5.5 cm. Abydos, D102. CMNH 1917-510.

The Egyptians normally ate while sitting on the floor or at low tables (figure 17). A typical dinner service consisted of a plate, a bowl, and a small mug or jug for liquids (figure 21). Eating utensils were very rare in ancient Egypt; even members of the royal family ate with their hands.

Under normal circumstances, the ancient Egyptians had as much food to eat as they desired. Only during times of extreme drought or the severest annual inundations was the country unable to feed its populace. The textual and representational evidence suggests that even the humblest peasants could find sufficient nourishment if only through fishing, hunting, fowling, and gathering.

The Egyptians consumed large amounts of meat and fowl. Beef, either boiled or roasted, was eaten regularly by the nobility. Country estate owners kept herds of oxen and cattle that were force-fed until the animals could barely walk; only then were they deemed ready for slaughter. Texts indicate that mutton, pig, and wild game, such as the hyena, were also part of the Egyptians' diet. The ancients raised geese and pigeons for food. They also hunted, killed, and consumed a wide variety of wild birds including herons, pelicans, cranes, and fourteen species of wild ducks and geese. Roast quail was regarded as a particular delicacy. Pelicans were kept as a source of eggs.

Local superstitions prohibited the consumption of certain species of fish in specific locations within Egypt. However, the great abundance of Nile fish proved an invaluable food source for the ancient Egyptians, who delighted in meals of catfish, mullet, bolti, and perch.

The rich soil along the Nile was ideally suited to the cultivation of vegetables and fruits. An Egyptian's meal might have included any number of local tuberous and root vegetables such as beets, sweet onions, radishes, turnips, and garlic. Lettuce was the most popular leafy vegetable. Legumes such as chickpeas, beans, lentils, and peas were also staples. A typical "Egyptian fruitbowl" would have been filled with figs, grapes, raisins, plums, dates, and watermelon.

Every meal had at least a small variety of breadstuffs. The Egyptians made bread from barley and emmer wheat. Their vocabulary contained over forty words for individual types of breads, cakes, and biscuits that specified differences in shape, the manner of baking, the variety of flour, and other ingredients including milk, eggs, fat, butter, honey, and fruit. Perhaps the most popular type of bread was a conical loaf baked in a mold, examples of which appear on representations of offering tables as early as Dynasty I (ca. 3100–2900 B.C.). The importance of bread in the Egyptians' diet exacted a toll on their teeth. Since most flour was ground on grinding stones made of friable rock, small abrasive particles often separated from the stone and combined with the flour. When this mixture was baked and eaten, considerable damage to the teeth resulted.

The Egyptians were among the great beer drinkers of antiquity. Their beer had an alcoholic content between 6.2 and 8.1 percent, roughly twice as potent as most modern brews. It was originally drunk from simple pottery tankards. Beginning in the New Kingdom (ca. 1539–1070 B.C.), however, the Egyptians adopted the Mesopotamian practice of drinking beer through metal tubes. This trend increased the potency of the beer and prevented the accidental drinking of any residual chaff. Ancient texts warn against the abuse of alcohol; to the Egyptians drunkenness was a reprehensible form of behavior.

The frequent depictions of grape arbors on tomb walls and the numerous wine vessels found throughout Egypt testify to the Egyptians' great love of wine. Because of its value, wine was normally limited to the Royal Court and the nobility; if the masses drank wine, they probably enjoyed it only during festivals. Most ancient wine was red, although there is some evidence that the Egyptians drank white wine as well. They recognized superior vintages and labeled wine jars with the year of production.

The Egyptians satisfied their sweet tooth with honey. Salt was used both to flavor and to preserve food.

Egyptologists know relatively little about the herbs and spices used in ancient times, but several well known in the modern world—including anise, cinnamon, cumin, dill, fennel, and thyme—may have existed in Pharaonic Egypt.

Entertainment and Recreation

The Egyptians were a fun-loving people who filled their leisure hours with pleasant diversions. Among the aristocracy, formal banquets provided an opportunity for feasting, drink, music, and conversation. Scantily clad maidens offered guests carefully prepared victuals and drinks and poured water over their hands when necessary. For the occasion, the hosts brought out their most impressive tableware, including finely crafted stone and faience drinking goblets and highly polished metal vessels (figures 22 and 23). Occasionally the celebrants overindulged. Two New Kingdom wall paintings show unfortunate party guests no longer able to hold down their food.

The most elegant banquets always featured a small orchestra. Stringed instruments such as harps, lyres, and lutes were a standard element of any Egyptian musical performance. Both long and short double flutes appear in many orchestral scenes; oboes, trumpets, and an instrument resembling a modern clarinet were also known in antiquity. Percussionists favored drums, tambourines, and small ivory clappers, sometimes carved in the form of human hands (figure 24).

Music pervaded all aspects of ancient Egyptian life. Shepherds and field hands sometimes worked to the

22. *Jug with a lotus-decorated handle.*

Bronze. Height 8.8 cm; diameter 6 cm. Early Dynasty XVIII (ca. 1479–1425 B.C.). Abydos, D116. CMNH 1917-54.

melody of a flutist or to the rhythm of ivory clappers. In certain religious ceremonies a worshiper, usually—although not always—a woman, would shake a bronze or copper rattle called a sistrum (figure 25). The sound was produced by tiny metal disks strung across one or more strands of taut wire. Sistra usually bore at least one image of the goddess Hathor and may have originally been used in her cult rituals.

Hunting, fowling, and fishing enjoyed great popularity among the nobility and perhaps among labor-

23. *Bowl.*

Bronze. Height 3.5 cm; diameter 15.3 cm. Early Dynasty XVIII (ca. 1479–1425 B.C.). Abydos, D116. CMNH 1917-53.

ers as well. Hunters used the bow and arrow for most game such as ibex, gazelles, wild cattle, ostriches, and hares. Tomb paintings show that Egyptian sportsmen might also test their accuracy with a throw stick, a lasso, or a weighted rope similar to the South American bolo. If a wounded animal temporarily escaped, the hunter would let loose one or more hunting dogs that would pursue the creature until it fell. Fowling and fishing were carried out in low papyrus skiffs that plied the marshlands bordering the Nile. The fowler, often holding a live bird as a decoy, usually felled his prey with a throw stick. Some illustrations show the fowler armed with a bow. Fishermen used long, double-barbed spears.

The Egyptians took great delight in their pets. At

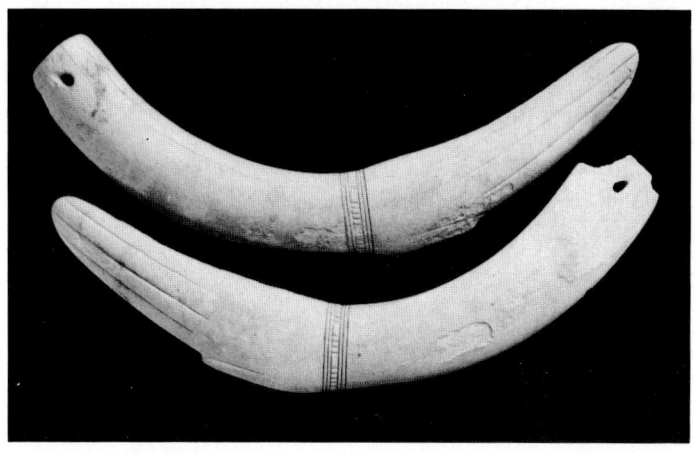

24. *Clappers.*
Ivory with black paste inlay.
Length 25 cm; width 3.6 cm.
Early Dynasty XVIII (ca.
1479–1425 B.C.). Abydos,
D116. CMNH 1917-8 and 9.

home, on the hunt, and at work, the dog *(tjesem)* was the Egyptians' most popular animal companion, and many families showed a marked affection for them. People adorned them with collars, buried them with elaborate ritual, and gave them affectionate names such as Good Herdsman, Ebony, and Son of the Moon. Tomb paintings and surviving skeletons show considerable variation in canine types, from a small animal resembling a contemporary Welsh corgi to a wolf-like "pariah dog." For hunting, the Egyptians preferred slender hounds, some with pendant ears and straight tails and others with short, curly tails and pointed, upright ears. Cats were not domesticated until Dynasty XI (ca. 2025–1979 B.C.). Two species lived in ancient Egypt: the short-eared *Felis ochreata* and the

25. Partial sistrum with the face of Hathor, the goddess associated with music, decorating the top of the handle. Bronze. Height 16.2 cm; width 4.5 cm. Late Period (ca. 664–332 B.C.). Provenience unknown. CMNH 9074-2251.

Felis chaus with its characteristic long ears, sharp nose, and wide tail. The ancient word for the housecat was the onomatopoeic *miw*. Monkeys, imported into Egypt from sub-Sahara Africa, were luxury pets, restricted to the homes of the wealthy.

In the quiet of their home, Egyptian family members had access to a number of board games. The most popular and long-lasting was *senet* ("passing"), played by all strata of society from kings to simple commoners. The *senet* board was usually carved or painted on one of the long sides of a rectangular box, which had sliding compartments to store the playing pieces (figure 26). The game was played by two people who moved their pieces along a field of thirty squares arranged in three rows of ten squares each. The length of a move was determined by casting either a series of flattened marked sticks or the large knucklebone of an animal. Although Egyptologists have attempted to reconstruct the rules of ancient *senet*, the details of play are still unknown. The object of the game seems to have been to negotiate all of one's pieces along the course of the board before the opponent could do so.

In literate households, reading proved a restful diversion. Egyptologists estimate that no more than 2 to 5 percent of the ancient population could read, but literacy was by no means restricted to the nobility. Many of the residents of the workers' village at Deir el-Medina could read and write. Certainly versions of Egyptian "classics" like the Middle Kingdom *Tale of Sinuhe* were available to those capable of enjoying and understanding them. Indeed, the most complete version of *Sinuhe* was discovered by archaeologists at Deir el-Medina.

Not all Egyptian leisure activity was so restrained. Many villages had brothels. Ancient texts warned

26. Game piece, possibly from a senet game, decorated with the face of a Bes-image, one of a group of protective deities of the household, often associated with music.

Faience. Height 1.2 cm; diameter 1.3 cm. Early Dynasty XVIII (ca. 1479–1425 B.C.). Abydos, D116. CMNH 1917-538.

young men about the dangers inherent in frequenting such places, but these admonishments were not always followed. An illustrated papyrus, now in the collection of the Turin Museum, shows one evening's activities within a bordello, probably located near Deir el-Medina. At least as early as Dynasty XVIII, the Egyptians imported opium marketed through Cyprus. Although it was used for medicinal purposes, it also functioned as a dream-inducing narcotic. Similarly the *Nymphaea* lotus (actually a lily), so common in Egyptian iconography, has a strong psychoactive effect. Although the ancients may not have been aware of this, the ubiquitous presence of the lotus at banquets as well as in the scene of the Deir el-Medina brothel suggests otherwise.

Popular Religion

Although religion pervaded all aspects of life in ancient Egypt, a mere handful of people had direct access to the gods, who were thought to dwell in great temples. Only priests and the king were permitted into a temple's inner recesses. Nobles might enter the temple forecourt, but they could go no farther. Commoners, such as the workers of Deir el-Medina, had to content themselves with occasional glimpses of their gods at one of the great state festivals, such as the Feast of Opet when Amun, the supreme state god, left his temple at Karnak for a brief visit at the nearby Luxor temple.

Pious Egyptians of modest social rank *were* able to worship at small local temples or sanctuaries. There they left inscribed statues and stelae proclaiming their devotion to a particular divinity. Several small temples that flourished near Deir el-Medina included those dedicated to Amun, Hathor, and King Amenhotep I and his mother Ahmes-Nofretari, both of whom were honored as the patrons of the town. The residents of Deir el-Medina believed the dead king was capable of oracular decisions and often came to his temple seeking advice in the resolution of a dispute.

Worship was not limited to formal religious structures. Residents of Egyptian villages practiced their own version of folk religion in their homes and at work. The French archaeologists who excavated Deir el-Medina unearthed a remarkable repertoire of objects demonstrating the deeply rooted beliefs of the resident families. One group of antiquities seemingly of a religious nature is a series of sculptures that may have been placed in the niches found in many Deir el-Medina homes. These pieces consist of a head and a schematically modeled upper body of a man or woman (figure 2). Although the precise meaning of these figures is not known, one theory holds that they represent a household deity that commemorated the family's ancestors. Certainly the veneration of deceased family members can be documented elsewhere at Deir el-Medina. A series of painted limestone stelae, probably inserted into the house walls, bares inscriptions invoking dead ancestors as "excellent spirits of [the sun god] Re."

Numerous amulets from the villages at Deir el-Medina and el-Amarna represent a host of minor gods whose primary function was the protection of the home and its inhabitants. One of these, a feminine creature, is a composite deity with the head and pregnant body of a hippopotamus, a lion's limbs, and a crocodile hanging down her back (figure 27). She is commonly called Taweret ("The Great One"), although a number of deities were shown with this unusual form. Her constant companion has the head, limbs, and tail of a male lion and the body of an achondroplastic dwarf (figure 28). Many minor gods, including Bes, Aha, and Hayet, are shown in this manner. Paintings of these male gods often appear on the walls of the antechambers at Deir el-Medina, where they watched over the

27. Schematic representation of Taweret incised and painted on a kohl tube.

Painted limestone. Height 9.3 cm; width 3 cm; length 5.8 cm. Early Dynasty XVIII (ca. 1479–1425 B.C.). Abydos, D116. CMNH 1917-2.

28. *Amulet depicting a Bes-image.*

Faience. Height 2.5 cm; width 1.1 cm. Early Dynasty XVIII (ca. 1479-1425 B.C.). Abydos, D116. CMNH 1917-40.

home, particularly at night. Both Taweret and her male counterpart also safeguarded pregnant women and the newly born.

Agricultural workers had occasion to pay homage to other unusual deities. Harvest and vintage scenes in Theban tombs show laborers toiling near small temporary shrines containing images of two snake deities, Renenutet, the Lady of the Harvest, and Meretseger, goddess of the Theban necropolis. The presence of one of these two deities guaranteed a successful harvest and protected the workers from snakes and scorpions.

The ancient Egyptians were, by nature, a superstitious lot. For example, they had a calendar that told them which days of the year were auspicious and which were adverse. Unlike a modern horoscope, which determines the advisability of activity for individuals, the Egyptian "magic calendar" applied to everyone. Thus

August 1 was considered very favorable and any effort was likely to succeed; October 17, however, was a day of misfortune when no journey was to be started. Although we do not know how pervasive belief in this system was in ancient Egypt, it is reasonable to guess that a reliance on magic may have appeared in any stratum of society.

Conclusion

Egyptian texts held that 110 years was the ideal age for death to occur. Infant mortality was probably quite high in ancient Egypt. However, if a baby survived infancy, it might look forward to a life expectancy of about 40 years for a male or about 30 years for a female. These figures would be slightly higher among the nobility. By Egyptian standards, anyone living to 50 would have been considered old. The Dynasty XVIII official Amenhotep, son of Hapu, was quite proud of reaching the age of 80, mentioning this accomplishment in the inscription on a statue that is today in the Cairo Museum.

Several ancient texts tell us that some Egyptians suffered from depression, especially during times of domestic unrest, and even contemplated suicide. Yet in surveying the evidence that survives from antiquity, we are left with the overall impression that most Egyptians loved life and were willing to overlook its hardships. Indeed, the perfect afterlife was merely an ideal version of their earthly existence. Only the travails and petty annoyances that bothered them in their lifetimes would be missing; all else, they hoped, would be as it was on earth.

Suggested Reading

Allam, Schafik. *Some Pages from Everyday Life in Ancient Egypt.* Vol. I, *Prism Archaeological Series.* Giza, Egypt: Foreign Cultural Information Department, 1985.

Bierbrier, Morris. *Tomb-Builders of the Pharaohs.* London: British Museum Publications, 1982.

Brier, Bob. *Ancient Egyptian Magic.* New York: William Morrow and Company, 1980.

Darby, William J., Paul Ghalioungui, and Louis Grivetti. *Food: The Gift of Osiris.* 2 vols. London: Academic Press, 1977.

Egypt's Golden Age: The Art of Living in the New Kingdom 1558–1085 B.C. (exhibition catalog edited by E. Brovarski, S.K. Doll, and Rita E. Freed). Boston: Museum of Fine Arts, 1982.

Hayes, William C. *The Scepter of Egypt: A Background for the Study of the Egyptian Antiquities in the Metropolitan Museum of Art.* 2 vols. Cambridge, Mass.: Harvard University Press, 1953 and 1959.

James, T.G.H. *Pharaoh's People: Scenes from Life in Imperial Egypt.* Chicago: University of Chicago Press, 1984.

Kamil, Jill. *The Ancient Egyptians: How They Lived and Worked.* London: David & Charles, 1976.

Lichtheim, M. *Ancient Egyptian Literature.* Berkeley: University of California Press, 1973–80. Vol. I, *The Old and Middle Kingdoms,* 1973.

Lucas, A. *Ancient Egyptian Materials and Industries.*

4th ed., revised and enlarged by J.R. Harris. London: Edward Arnold, 1962.

Manniche, Lisa. *Sexual Life in Ancient Egypt.* London: KPI, 1987.

Mertz, Barbara. *Red Land, Black Land: Daily Life in Ancient Egypt.* New York: Dodd, Mead & Company, 1978.

Montet, Pierre. *Everyday Life in the Days of Ramesses the Great.* Translated by A.R. Maxwell-Hyslop and Margaret S. Drower. London: Edward Arnold, 1958.

Romer, John. *Ancient Lives: Daily Life in Egypt of the Pharaohs.* New York: Holt, Rinehart, and Winston, 1984.

Stead, Miriam. *Egyptian Life.* London: British Museum Publications, 1986.

Acknowledgments

Front cover. Drawing by Linda A. Witt.
Figs. 1, 2, 5, and 15–17. Courtesy of The Brooklyn Museum.
Figs. 3, 4, 6–11, and 19–28. CMNH photographs by Melinda McNaugher.
Fig. 12. Line drawing adapted by Nancy Perkins from A. Badawy, *A History of Egyptian Architecture* (Berkeley: University of California, 1968), fig. 1.
Figs. 13 and 14. Line drawings adapted by Linda A. Witt from A. Badawy, *A History of Egyptian Architecture* (Berkeley: University of California, 1968), figs. 34 and 60.
Fig. 18. Courtesy of The Metropolitan Museum of Art, all rights reserved.